THE BUSINESS END OF PROCESS SERVICE

(RUNNING A PROCESS SERVICE COMPANY FROM THE GROUND UP)

By Bob Hill

Warning: This is not a manual on how to serve legal process. It is a manual on how to create and operate a full service process serving company from the bottom up, including business structure, equipment necessary, hardware and software tools, and marketing practices specific to the industry. Although the industry practices are given a general overview throughout the book, the various techniques, training, requirements, laws, regulations, and legal rules are only described in general terms as an introductory discussion to the civil process service profession. It is suggested that one take a course on civil process provided in your state which can usually be found in junior colleges, local law enforcement training courses, and state and national process serving associations.

TABLE OF CONTENTS

1.	WHAT THIS BOOK ISN'T	4
2.	MAKING MONEY AS A TRAINED MONKEY	6
3.	WHAT IS PROCESS SERVICE	8
4.	WHY START A PROCESS SERVING BUSINESS	12
5.	SETTING UP THE BUSINESS STRUCTURE	20
6.	WHAT'S IN A NAME?	27
7.	TRAINING	31
8.	PRICING AND QUALITY VERSUS QUANTITY	35
9.	MARKETING	43
10.	EQUIPMENT/SUPPLIES NEEDED	64
11.	DRESS AND APPEARANCE	70
12.	FINANCES AND TAXES	73
13.	KEEPING TRACK OF THINGS	78
14.	SETTING UP A DAILY ROUTINE	93
15.	THAT'S A WRAP	99

WHAT THIS BOOK ISN'T

Although the exciting world of process service is discussed and described in general terms throughout this book, let it be known that this is not about how to serve process. It is not about "tricks of the trade" or how to complete those difficult serves. It's not about how to properly complete a return of service. It's not about knowing all the rules and regulations regarding civil process. It's not about how to become a process server or to teach in any detail about process serving.

There are plenty of books out there that address the various scenarios, plans, devices, opportunities, and "slight of hand" for serving civil process. There are also thousands of experienced process servers in the business, some right there in your home town, that will be all to willing to share in their knowledge on how to get the job done. There are tons of training seminars, schools, online courses, certified instructors, books, codes, rules, and regulations that address how to properly complete returns of service, and how to properly serve court documents in accordance with whatever state or venue in which you are located.

Although there are plenty of things packed into this book regarding how to organize, automate, market, and operate a process serving business and are specific to the daily operations of a process serving company, as well as some things in here that could be applied to any small business, this is not the book that teaches you how get a "deadbeat dad" to open the front door of his dilapidated one bedroom apartment.

If that is what you are looking for, please put this book down, as this book is about making a process service company that runs quick, smooth, and clean allowing for greater profitability, working smarter not harder, and at the same time allowing you to have a life outside of the business so that the business doesn't take over your life. As is true with most all small businesses, if one is not organized and prepared, one finds oneself not running the business at all, but rather the business runs you.

MAKING MONEY AS A TRAINED MONKEY

Do you want to make some money on the side? Do you want to make enough money to pay for your living expenses and to have a comfortable life? Do you want to make so much money that you are tempted to burn it in the fireplace to warm your heart? Well, you can do it serving court documents. In fact, process serving is so easy to do and takes very little training and work experience that even a trained monkey can do it. Trust me, I know. I used to be a trained monkey, and now I run a small process serving and private investigative firm, making hundreds of thousands of dollars a year doing it. And if I can do it, so can you.

But how? Yes, of course, it didn't happen overnight. Nothing honest ever leads to quick upward mobility. It took several years of trial and error, and doing and not doing, before I figured out a few things that helped me go from renting a one bedroom apartment and driving a used, beat up pickup truck, to owning a nice home, driving a nice new car, living my lifestyle debt free, and being able to take the occasional vacation. I also did it without having to put forth a lot of capital upfront or rely on a rich old uncle to fund my ambitions.

Ten years it took to go from zero to sixty, but what I learned in ten years, you are going to know in just the few short hours you'll spend reading this book, because I am going to shortcut things for you. By the time you're finished, you'll not only be a trained monkey you'll be a smart one, too. And depending on your goals you'll either be able to quickly gain some extra income serving process, or change your life by making buckets full of money.

WHAT IS PROCESS SERVICE?

Legally speaking, process service is the delivery of writs or summons issued by and through a court or judicial venue upon a defendant or respondent of a civil lawsuit, or delivery of a subpoena to a witness. At times this can be as simple as your typical courier delivery, or as complex as an undercover drug bust.

Now there are those out there who would attempt to convince you that process service is difficult and technical, and requires a certain level of expertise. In *some* instances that would be true, especially when it comes to the proper completion of returns of service. In some instances delivering a court document could require a certain level of intrepidity and a degree of legerdemain (look it up). But for the vast majority of court documents to be delivered, all that is required is knowledge of the specific laws and rules set forth by the court for the proper execution (delivery) of court documents, and a little bit of common sense. For the vast majority of court documents to be delivered, a trained monkey could do it.

So here's the nuts and bolts of what a trained monkey does on a routine execution of a court document. A client will make contact either by phone or email and request that a court document be picked up at the courthouse (usually). The server then goes to the courthouse, picks up the specific court document for the certain law suit the client has briefed the server on, and then the server will go to the address where the court document is directed to be delivered to a specific person (usually). Upon the server's appearance at the service address, the server identifies himself/herself to whoever should answer the door at that service address, and then asks to see the person to whom the court documents are directed.

Usually, if the timing is right and the service address is current, the person to whom the court documents are directed will be present and will come to the front door. At that point the server will state the purpose for his appearance there (delivering court documents), and then hand the documents to the person to whom the court documents are directed. Then the server leaves, subsequently completes an affidavit of service, which would state the date, time, place and to whom the documents were left with, and this affidavit would be filed at the courthouse thereby making it officially known in the court records that the court documents had been delivered (served).

Most of the time the above scenario is what occurs. The process (no pun intended) is actually a little more technical than described, but this is the general gist of it for the purposes of our discussion here. There are courses out there that are sanctioned by the various courts across the nation, and are taught by numerous private schools, junior colleges, and process serving associations that can teach the more technical aspects of process serving, along with the specific laws for each particular venue in which court documents are served. We strongly advise that before starting in the process serving industry that you take a course on it, and in some venues or states, it is required that you do so in order to even qualify for a license or a certification (if your state requires one). That way you will become familiar with the particular rules and laws that govern how you are to "execute" service of process as each state has different, although, similar rules governing how court documents are to be served.

WHY START A PROCESS SERVING BUSINESS

There are an endless supply of ideas, products, services, and gimmicks one could use to start a business and make a profit. You name it, you can make a business out of it. But the list of businesses begins to narrow as one considers where their own passions, interests, mental and physical limitations, academic training, life experience, work experience, moral and philosophical beliefs, family and social structure, and financial budget are realistically situated.

From my perspective, one can do or be anything they wish, and can get involved in anything they want if they had the desire. There is simply no excuse, and in a free society there are no true limits. That, my friends, is reality, despite the theory that most people believe about themselves – that they are limited.

So, for those of you reading this that are skeptical as to

whether this is a service you could create a business that is profitable and satisfying, and can fit it into whatever limitations you feel you may have in life, I urge you to read on. When you're done, if you're not convinced this is for you, then keep looking for something else. You will find what is right for you. For the rest of you, this could be the start of a fun, rarely boring, hardly routine, somewhat flexible, and potentially lucrative business that could grow as big or stay as small as you would like it, and you will be able to do it with a very small investment in money and time compared to many careers and business opportunities available. You could pick up some extra spending money, you could make a solid income, or you could take it to the max. How fast and how far you go would be up to you, just as in any other business one could start up.

You can start in the process serving industry with very little financial investment, no expensive products to manufacture, no inventory to keep on stock, no complicated business ventures with fast talking, high-powered business executives, no slick, new ideas, nothing to invent, patent, copyright, or mass produce. All it takes is a little motivation, a little time, or as much as you are willing to put into it, and a minimum of investment capital that just about anyone could find in their own personal bank account, or the cushions of their sofa. Now how's that for a start-up business?

Secondly, process service is the type of business one can start up part-time, while still working at a full-time job. If one simply puts forth the effort, after working for the man, in just a few hours after work, one can work for themselves – and probably make just as much money in those few hours after work as they did the entire day working their full-time job. And the beauty of it is, you're the boss. You decide which assignments you want to take, and in most instances, you can decide when to complete the assignments, how you complete them, and whether you want to do them at all. You could go at your own speed, slow or fast. Make as much money as you want, just as long as you hustle for it as fast as you want. If you really want to make it, put your nose to it. If you just want beer money, then go at your own leisure, and enjoy the cold brew once you collect your pay.

Since delivering process often entails delivering court documents to individuals at their homes, it is very easy to do this while working a nine-to-five job. Although you are working all day, most likely the soon-to-be-defendant in a lawsuit or a respondent in a divorce is most likely also working a nine-to-five job. So, once you're off from your nine-to-five job, all you have to do is gather up your assignments, map out your route, and start knocking on doors in the late afternoon or early evening. Or you could flip it around, and deliver process in the early morning before everyone goes off to work, or deliver the court documents on the weekend (provided there are no legal prohibitions against serving on the weekends in your particular state).

Thirdly, process service is a profession that requires very little training. As I often joke, a trained monkey could serve papers. But you do have to be trained, whether you are a monkey or not.

Yet, the training, depending on the state, can be quite simple or even on-the-job, so to speak. In the state of Texas, where I began, my training came from two sources; previous experience as a law enforcement agent, but also through specialized courses I took at a local junior college so that I could familiarize myself with the specific laws, and practices for completing the "execution" and the paperwork. But one can also obtain valuable training on process service through national associations, such as the National Association of Professional Process Servers (NAPPS), which is also a great networking organization, and an excellent source for obtaining local assignments in your area from other process servers and attorneys from all over the world, or from state associations that often hold relatively inexpensive training seminars on how to serve process. There are also endless sources for taking online courses that in some states qualify for continuing education credits in those states where process service is well-regulated, such as is the case in Texas, New York, Florida, and California. And did I mention, all of these training courses are typically very inexpensive, and not very lengthy. The last "refresher" course I took, which is the same course required for new licensees, I spent one day in class. And the course was taught on a Saturday, meaning it didn't interrupt my work schedule, and I still had Sunday to spend with my family. Now how's that for learning about a new trade, perhaps even getting qualified for any required license in your state, and doing it cheaply. Usually, the cost is a couple hundred dollars or less.

Lastly, process service is one of those best kept secrets. It's an industry that makes millions of dollars a year, and yet very few people even know what a process server is or does for a living.

It's the sort of business that makes good money if you just

apply yourself, do a good job, and are responsive to your clients' needs, and, most importantly, what I have discovered having gone through two economic recessions since entering the process serving business, is that it is somewhat "recession proof". So few know about it, and yet it is a constant steady stream of income for me, my family, and the servers that work for me. I have many competitors, but hardly anyone knows about them. Process servers don't have ads on television, we're not household names, and only our clients really know about us. But while the car dealerships are suffering from low sales, and the banks are collapsing from giving out bad loans, and the real estate agents are starving because no one else is employed or invested enough to be able to buy a house, in an economic downturn, our demand goes up, and so does our revenue. It may sound harsh, even almost parasitic, but when things go bad, a process server is usually the bearer of those bad tidings. I don't personally wish anyone an ill-fate, but life is filled with bad things that happen, even to good people. As a process server our job is merely to deliver the bad news, just like the postman delivers a letter. And it is really nothing more than that; a delivery, nothing personal, and all professional.

Process serving typically has repeat customers. Your customer market leads are lawyers – more specifically, the lawyers' legal assistants. And once you get your first assignment with one of them, execute the assignment professionally, and promptly, and charge a reasonable rate, you will most likely keep them as a customer for the next lawsuit they file where they will need to have the court documents delivered to the defendant or a subpoena delivered to a witness in the middle of any one of the many ongoing lawsuits they might have ongoing. There are some attorneys I have known for fifteen years, and still call upon my company to serve their court documents. Many of those attorneys have become good friends, and also trusted advisors at times when I or my family needed legal advice of our own.

The typical process serving assignment might only net you $50-$75 dollars for that one assignment, but the repeat business over time from that one attorney could over the course of several years net you tens, perhaps hundreds of thousands of dollars. And that's just from one customer.

What's more, that one and/or first attorney-client, could refer you to someone else working in his/her law firm, or his secretary or paralegal could refer you as well to some other attorney, secretary, or paralegal at yet another law firm, and now you have free of charge for the advertising yet another customer. And you did it by word-of-mouth, which is the cheapest and bestest way to market for new clients. It costs nothing and is the easiest sale you'll ever make because someone else did the marketing and closed the deal for you. The next thing you know, without even really trying, you could have a heavy handful of customers, growing your business organically, without having done any advertising, marketing, schmoozing, networking, or door-knocking. Once the buzz is on the street about you, you'll have no shortage of customers, and you'll be on your way to being busier than you probably want to be in a very short time.

SETTING UP THE BUSINESS

There are numerous and varied ways of setting up the business in terms of structure, licensing, permits, etc. Depending on your situation one can structure a business as a sole proprietorship, dual proprietorship, limited liability partnership, a corporation, limited liability corporation, etc…you get the point.

Talk to attorneys, accountants, other business professionals, and each will tell you something different. One will tell you, keep it simple and do a sole proprietorship. Another will say start up a corporation to protect your personal assets. What do you do? Who's right?

No one.

Not totally, and not all of the time in any given situation.

Now under the advice of our own advisors, we must

categorically state that you should not take our wisdom or direction as legal advice. And we must urge that you consult a competent attorney regarding these matters if you have any questions. They can best advise you as to what is the best entity to formulate given your unique situation.

But it can be as easy or as hard as you need it to be to fit your circumstances. We just suggest and describe the different types of entities out there.

Now if you are starting out, and I am assuming that is what you are doing, otherwise you wouldn't be reading this, then taking the easy route, at least in the beginning, could be one of the ways to go.

In the State of Texas, where my company is based, all it takes to begin operating most businesses is an assumed name in the form of a "doing business as" sole proprietorship. One simply goes to the court house, fills out a one page application, pays a simple fee that is usually under $20.00, depending on the county you reside, and now you have a sole proprietorship. You own a company name, too. At least you can operate in that county with a business using that "assumed" company "name" you placed on the county application form. It's inexpensive, quick, and gives you a little bit of legitimacy as a business. An assumed name does not give you any legal protections or tax benefits, but at least you can operate your company under a name other than the one given to you by your parents. Nothing wrong with using your own name, but most professional attorneys would probably prefer doing business with someone who has at least a "doing business as" sole proprietorship.

I started that way, and it made the regulatory process simplistic. There were no major fees, no governmental compliances that involved additional fees, and I could focus on running the business as opposed to being a liaison between the company and various levels of municipal, county, state and federal government. It is also, in my opinion, not necessary to form anything more complicated unless you have considerable personal assets such as real property, investment savings, or other things of real value that could be taken from you should something go awry. And, even so, that is what a good error and omissions policy is good for (more on insurance later in the book).

A partnership is another entity that if you are going into this business with a friend or associate it is also relatively simple. In

Texas a general partnership is arranged in the same way as a sole proprietorship and is sometimes called a dual proprietorship. Same form, just two or three or more individuals are filing together under one assumed name when a partnership is filed in its very basic formula. There are variations on a partnership, though, some opt to start a limited liability partnership, which can be considerably more complicated and costly, too, but this can also provide some legal protection to the partners.

As a suggestion, though, whatever the formula used for a partnership, it would be best to also have a written agreement between the partners as to who is responsible for what, what are the percentages of ownership of the company, what assets will each partner bring into the company to create and maintain the company, and what happens with all the assets, equipment, and debts should the partnership dissolve at some future time. For a partnership agreement to be binding, we strongly suggest you consult a competent attorney to make sure everything is legitimate and that everything has been contemplated before the partnership is official. In the beginning everyone in a partnership may be on good terms, but if the partnership fails to maintain cohesion and camaraderie, most likely any "oral" agreements will fall by the side of the road, and then everyone will be hard pressed to agree to anything when the partnership dissolves.

You could also set up a standard "for profit" corporation. This also provides certain legal protections for the owners as does a limited liability partnership, but also carries with it certain complications. For example, the owners (or principals) would be considered employees of the corporation, even though it might just be you doing everything and running everything. Since a corporation is a "stand-alone" entity separate from an individual all assets of the corporation are the property of the corporation and not the individual principals or the employees. And the employees themselves, right on up to the CEO or president (which when starting out would be you) have to be put on the payroll. As one can see, this can be good in terms of separating your personal assets from the corporation just in case something occurs that leads to a liability or a lawsuit against the company, but once you form a corporation it becomes a bit more complicated to manage the "business end" of things, and I have not even mentioned everything else that a corporation entails. The list of managerial responsibilities grows exponentially when comparing an entity such as a sole proprietorship to a corporation. So, it would be very wise to consult a competent attorney or accountant about forming a corporation just to make sure you fully understand the rules and laws for your state.

The last legal entity for a company is what is called the limited liability company. This form of entity typically has the legal protections of a corporation without the various complications of managing the "business end" of a corporation. There are still some things you have to do to maintain good standing of an LLC with the state authorities, but LLC's are far less complicated than a corporation. And again, most states have a yearly fee to renew and to maintain a good standing with the state.

So, as you can see there are various ways of formally structuring your business and even within the different types described there are subcategories as well as other ways to structure your business so that you can use a combination of these entities together. But for ease of purpose, just starting out in a spare bedroom of your home, without any clients, without a lot of "venture capital", without much in the way of business equipment or a need to protect personal assets, an assumed name would be the simplest, cheapest and easiest way to go. Later, when the business grows, and you assume the hiring of employees, or have to rent or decide to own an office building/space, then you can consider changing the structure to something more complicated and something that can provide protection.

But again, I cannot stress it enough: Do your research and consult competent legal advice if you are uncertain about any aspect of the law when it comes to formulating your company's business structure.

WHAT'S IN A NAME?

It may not seem important to some, but having a business name can be crucial. Not only does it give you legitimacy, as opposed to calling your business, "Joe Smith, Process Server," it can give you brand recognition and a marketing hook.

Don't get me wrong, just going out there with business cards that say Joe Smith, Process Server, may be fine. Especially if you want to be identified as just a regular "Joe" who serves papers. There's really nothing wrong with it. Depending on the type of clients you might want to attract, that might be perfect.

But that is also the point I am making. How you name the business will identify the type of business you have and it will shape the psychology that the name inevitably employs upon you, any future employees, your clients' perceptions of the type of business or service you are providing, and whether you or the company will grow up, out, or sideways.

The name of my company started out as Record Time Retrieval. It was catchy for what the identity of the business was back then, which, actually, was not a full-service process service and private investigative firm. At the inception, Record Time Retrieval was a records retrieval company that basically served subpoenas to obtain business and medical records that could be used by attorney-clients in their lawsuits. Records retrieval is a business within the legal support industry all by itself, and can be a money-maker, too, if you have good cash-flow, and a meticulous mindset. Now the name Record Time Retrieval fit the business at that time. We retrieved records in record time. It was perfect, and, much to the point gave us an identity. Clients knew what we did and that we did it quickly ... in Record Time.

But over time, we changed the type of service we wanted to provide from records retrieval to process service and then we added private investigations. As the owner (and at the time the only "employee"), I was more inclined to work on process service as I had a previous law enforcement background, so the quick turnaround on assignment completions that process service entails was a much better fit for me as a "worker". We still occasionally do records retrieval, but we are predominately process service and private investigations now. The only problem, though, as the service changed to suit my passions and my personality, was that the company's name was Record Time Retrieval & Investigations (at that point).

We got a little stuck because we already had clients, business cards, a website, stationary, etc. Changing all of that would have confused existing clients and cost the company money. So, as you can see, just from my own experience (or lack thereof) the importance of a company name, especially if you change out your services. Eventually, although we are still formally Record Time Retrieval & Investigations we now just present it as Record Time so that it still gives us some brand recognition.

And that's what you should think about when coming up with a name. If your focus is to be a process serving company that is very professional, then a name like Professional Process might work. If it is important to have your family name on your "shingle", then by all means, call it Thompson's Civil Process. Just remember, the name says it all, and it gives your company a distinct identity as well as (especially, if it has a recognizable, catchy name) a marketable slant that perhaps gives you an edge over your competition. Think hard and long on it, and what you want the company to represent because you do not want to go through the contortions my company went through when we changed services, but then struggled with how we wanted to represent that change later on down the road.

TRAINING

So how do you get trained to do this sort of business? I mean, not just the business end of things, but the nuts and bolts of how to serve legal process. There are numerous options and depending on your state, there may be certain required training you have to undergo.

When I first started out, I had previous law enforcement experience that was helpful in terms of at least knowing what process service was and generally speaking how to go about it. But my law enforcement experience came from a federal background as I was a criminal investigator for one of the military branches. So I knew very well how to execute federal search warrants, subpoenas, and summons. But when I left the government to go serve civil process in the State of Texas, I was not entirely familiar with the rules or the various forms used and how to complete them.

At that time, which was the early 1990's there really wasn't any training courses specifically designed for private process servers. So, instead, I attended a short peace officers course at a local community college. The cost was fairly inexpensive and I became exposed to a great many rules and the various writs and how to complete them. It was by no means comprehensive and complete in terms of knowledge, but it allowed me to move forward.

Since then, there have been certain changes in the laws in Texas that now require a private process service class be taken in order to be allowed by the state to even begin serving civil process. These courses are private courses specifically designed for process servers and are typically sponsored by the state association, the Texas Process Servers Association, or other state recognized private instructors. At the present time the one I recommend if you are going to serve papers in Texas would be through the Process Servers Network. You can locate them online at http://www. psntexas.com. The instructor is state certified and the class material is well-presented. Currently, experienced process servers are required to take a renewal course every three years in Texas. I find that each time I have attended a renewal course through Process Servers Network I learn at least one new thing (or more) of which I had not been previously aware.

There are several other schools, too, all of which are sanctioned by the state of Texas, to include courses taught by the Texas Process Servers Association, the Texas Association of Licensed Investigators, and the Houston Young Lawyers Association, just to name a few. You can locate a list of current certified training schools through the Texas Process Servers Review Board, which is administrated by the Texas Supreme Court. The website for the PSRB is www.courts.state.tx.us/psrb/psrbhome.asp.

If you are serving process in another state, then I suggest you contact your local state association or speak with a clerk at the courthouse who might point you in the right direction in terms of where you might be able to find the training and/or if there are any requirements for training in your state.

Another way to learn how to serve civil process would be to go to work for another process server willing to show you the correct methods. There are thousands of process serving companies throughout the United States that are large enough to require more than just one process server, and it is possible that you could take a position with one of these companies early on just so you can learn how to properly deliver court documents (and to also see if you actually like process service as a profession) before going off on your own.

Last, if you are one of those people that would rather learn on your own, there is nothing wrong with that, but it is important to become familiar with the laws and rules for your state as they apply to process service. You will find the requirements under the law are usually found within your state's civil rules of procedure. Also, you can find books on line through various outlets authored by process servers and private investigators on how to serve court documents and also learn various "tricks of the trade", as well.

PRICING AND QUALITY VERSUS QUANTITY

So how much should you charge for your services? It is an excellent question, and one that the answer varies depending on who you ask. I have heard that the "golden rule" for pricing how much to serve for a single instrument (one court document) should be based on a competitive rate with, if not the same as, what the local sheriff or constable's office charges for the same exact assignment. But then I have experienced in my business dealings with other process server's a variance in the price that in some instances swings wildly from one extreme to the other.

So what's the answer? In my opinion there really is not a hard and fast rule, but rather an amalgamation of factors that play into pricing. First, you do have to consider what the sheriff or the constable charges for serving papers to a small degree. Since they are traditionally the ones that served civil process before private process servers came along, there is an opinion out there that they have set the standard. They may not be setting the standard in terms of quality or speed of service, but for some reason the standard has been or was set by the local shire reeves (this is the original pronunciation for the sheriff from the old English dialect). But I would not consider them the only factor by a long shot, after all, the reason private process serving has become an industry at all is because the volume of work available is so enormous that the quality and speed of the service derived from the sheriff or the constables is substandard, most especially in large metropolitan areas (markets). This is not because the sheriff or the constables are terrible at what they do, but rather they simply do not have the staffing for the most part.

So, consider what they charge the public for service of process, but also factor in some other things, too. First, would be fuel costs. Distance traveled to deliver a paper should be factored into your pricing as it relates to fuel costs. If one has to travel thirty miles to deliver a court document then pricing should be considered to reflect that cost. It has been said that for every dollar cost per gallon of gas, one should factor a cost of $5.00 for the service. Now, that is not to say that if gas costs $1.00 per gallon that you should charge $5.00. No, what it says is that if gas costs $3.00 per gallon, then your fuel costs for the average process serving assignment should be $15.00 plus the cost of actually doing the service.

You might be scratching your head, so let me give you an example. It is usually recognized that if you have an overall price of $60.00 per court document you serve in your local market, $30.00 should be for the actual serving part of the assignment. $30.00 to cover your time to go from your office to the service address. Then you have $15.00 to cover fuel costs. Now you are at $45.00. But wait, you say, that doesn't add up to $60.00, and you're correct. The remaining $15.00 is factored in for your office expenses, such as paper and other office supplies, insurance, utilities, advertising costs, and taxes. Taxes? But process serving usually doesn't come along with sales tax, you say. No, it doesn't but you have to factor in your income tax withholdings, property tax, franchise tax, and other sorts of government levees placed upon your business in accordance with the laws of your city, county, and state governments.

So then, what happens if fuel costs go up? Well, if a gallon of gas goes from $3.00 to $4.00 then it would mean that you should probably consider raising your price from $60.00 to $65.00.

Speed of delivery is another factor. It is one thing if you have a court document that needs to be served. It is another thing if your client needs it served right now. Charge a rush fee for that. Why? Well, beyond the obvious, let me put it to you this way. If you have five routine papers you need to serve and four of them are all situated in one general locale, but then you have the fifth one needs to be served that day ... no, that very instant and it is on the other side of town, thereby taking you away from the $240.00 you will make off of the four other papers, it just makes good business sense that the client needs to understand (and they typically do) that a premium charge needs to be assessed. After all, you are now delaying four other papers from being served just to insure that one gets done. Don't be shy about charging for a rush. Sure, if you want to score points with the client, then perhaps you might occasionally consider not charging the rush fee. But do that too often and you will find yourself working harder for a lot less profit than you can reasonably expect to make.

Level of difficulty of the assignment is another key factor.

What if you have to deliver court documents on a military installation? What if you have wait two hours at a particular location for the defendant/witness to appear so you can serve them? What if you have to develop some sort of complex operation in order to find yourself in front of the defendant/witness because they have been or are known to evade service? These things should sometimes be factored into the equation on a case by case basis.

Number of documents to be served. This is another area to keep in mind. Now I have seen this vary from server to server. If, as we continue with the pricing example of $60.00 per paper, it turns out you have two different types of documents to deliver to the same individual, should you charge for that extra document? Some servers don't. Others do but only at half the price of the first document ($30.00), and others charge full price for the second document ($60.00). In terms of pricing second instruments (or second documents), to charge or not to charge is the question. If you ask your client, especially those who operate in family law, they do not like to be charged for second instruments for the obvious reason that the costs go up for them. But in the case of family law, where it is typical you will see second and third and sometimes fourth instruments, there is the issue of your time for completing the various affidavits of service that come with those extra documents, there is the factoring in that should you forget to deliver one of those extra documents that this could mean the difference between a court appearance or a cancellation because you forgot to serve that extra document, and you have to consider that your liability towards your client goes up considerably if you fail to complete or fail to serve everything properly. What I have mostly experienced is that second instruments are charged at half the going rate of a first instrument. Very few servers charge nothing for the extra document, and those that charge full price very rarely get the business or get it from a very loyal constituent of clients.

At the end of the day, I will provide you with two prevailing rules of capitalist economics. First, charge what you can afford. Second, charge based on demand.

For the first rule, don't set your price so low that your expenses eat up all your profit (hence you have no profit). As with the fuel costs and other expenses of running a business, if you decide to price things so low in an attempt to undercut your competitors, you may find yourself out of business and possibly in foreclosure or bankruptcy while your competitors are still running strong. Secondly, and this will play upon the second rule to a degree. If you do price yourself too low, you might find yourself so busy that you cannot perform quality service, and eventually this leads to mistakes, missed deadlines on court appearances for your clients, and then the eventual exodus of your entire book of clients.

Which leads to the second rule, that the charge should be what the market demands. If the typical going rate for service of one court document in your market is $60.00, and you charge $55.00 the price will lead to demand for your service based on the lower price. But if you get too busy because you are cheaper, then you will get over loaded with assignments and provide poor service. That, and you will also work yourself to an early grave. But, if you keep your price competitive at $60.00 or even a little higher, you will gain a share of the market amongst your local competitors, considering everyone is charging the same relative price, or you might be working less if you charge $65.00, but end up making the same amount of money as your competitors or perhaps even more. So what you would rather do? Work harder for less money per assignment? Or do you prefer to work less for the same amount of money, be tanned and rested, and not be overloaded with too many assignments, and be able to provide superior service to your current book of clients, who in turn tout your good name and superior performance to others who might have a need for your services? In other words, do you want to do quantity or do you want to quality of work? Think about it.

MARKETING

It truly is all about the sale. Without marketing, without selling, you have no business. This is the most critical part of your day-to-day operations, especially if you are just starting out and have no process to deliver.

Getting clients and then keeping them is what you must do every day. I keep telling myself this all the time. When I forget to do this, I am reminded of it within a very short period because I will notice a drop in business, and a decrease in my accounts receivables. But how could this be when process service typically has repeat customers, i.e., attorneys who are constantly filing lawsuits? It is a common axiom. Even if you have a repeat client-base, if you fail to give good customer service, face-time, or excellent service, someone else will, and you'll be out in the cold. And even if you do provide good customer service and an excellent product, eventually something else happens with the client in terms of them going out of business, moving, retiring, and/or (heaven forbid) passing through the pearly gates.

All of these things and more have happened to me during the tenure of running my business. And don't think you're so perfect that it won't happen to you. I have had some clients for over ten years, suddenly drop off for various reasons, and replacing them with another client is not so simple. The adage it takes three months to get and keep a customer and three minutes to lose them is very much a reality. So don't rest for too long. Marketing and advertising are critical and constant and paramount.

That's why I treat marketing in a two-pronged approach. Always look for new clients while at the same time treating your current client's like royalty. That's not to say you should kiss the ground they walk on, but you should continue to market the clients you already have while looking for others at the same time. Be like a shark and never stop swimming ... or you will die.

Okay, so you ask, how do you do that? Well, for one thing, you cannot market clients by being a secret agent of sorts. If no one knows you're there to do the work, then it is as if you really are not there to do the work. Get the word out and let everyone know you are there.

Here is a list of the types of things I have done to get the word out that I am serving legal process:

1. Advertisement in local bar association newsletter. What is key here is that you are being industry specific and targeting one demographic – law firms.

2. Yellow pages and business pages (even just a one-liner is better than a no-liner).

3. Order some business cards and place them in the hands of every court clerk you encounter. Oftentimes an attorney or a private individual is at the courthouse filing their lawsuit and they don't know a process server. If asked, and they have one of your business cards, the court clerk will be just like a sales referral for you (of course, it helps that you are friendly and smile when you make acquaintances with the clerks. It helps even better if you bring them some cookies or some donuts every once in a while, too).

4. Obtain a copy of the local bar association membership listing or directory. Identify those attorneys who do litigation,

whether it is family law, personal injury, commercial litigation, debt collection, etc. Once identified, order up some postcards with your company name, the phone number, and state on the postcard that your company provides process service. This is a numbers game, so you will have to send out several hundred or several thousand of these postcards before you get a client. But once you do and you complete an assignment, you will most likely have that client for years to come and it will defray the costs of the postcards. The rule of five applies here, mind you. What is the rule of five? This rule states that a potential customer may have to see your advertisement (in this case a post card) at least five times before they actually consider hiring you or purchasing your product.

  5. Website. The internet is rapidly replacing things that are in hard copy print. Even if you just have one single webpage that you personally constructed using an inexpensive web hosting template, it's better than having no presence on the net. We started with a very inexpensive web hosting template. For only a few hundred dollars, I drafted my own website when we first started out. It wasn't the greatest, didn't have all the bells and whistles, and over time I had to change things, find experts to enhance the

"searchability" and appearance, but if one is going to do business in the 21st Century one must eventually invest in a website.

Now, if you are just starting out a website might not draw in a lot of work if it is just a basic one that you set up yourself without any "search engine optimization" or all that fancy computer "stuff" (as I call it), but get it started. Over time, as the company begins to bring in steady revenue, you can always get the right service to upgrade and enhance the website so that customers can find it whenever they conduct a search on the internet for a process server. What little I do know, as I am not an expert in website design, the best thing one can do is to optimize the website so that search engines can easily pick it up. This requires the ability to be able to know how to submit your website to the various search engines, like google, yahoo, etc. I rely on a website hosting service to handle this for our company. Also, to draw traffic to the website, consider exchanging links with other businesses as this is known to draw traffic toward your website. But first and foremost, get the site up and running at the very least. And then, if you have the funds, hire a "qualified" web professional who knows how to submit your website to the search engines and knows how to push traffic towards your website. And what I mean by qualified, in my opinion, is ask someone who already has a website where the website is getting traffic on it. The last thing you want to do is spend a lot of money to have someone set up a website for you and they promise to get the internet traffic to it, too, and then you find out that person or company doesn't know what they are doing and they are just taking you for a ride on the information superhighway at your expense.

6. NAPPS. The National Association of Professional Process Servers is by its name a national association. And it is an excellent conduit for obtaining assignments from other process servers and law firms, especially those that are outside your state or your city. There are other excellent benefits to being a member, but this association is very affordable to join, provided you are eligible, and the return on your investment is sometimes ten to twenty times what you put into it. Our main office in San Antonio receives at least a hundred assignments or more every year, which may not seem like a lot, and one certainly cannot make a living just on that amount, but a hundred assignments is a lot more than zero assignments. Check on the internet for www.napps.org for eligibility requirements, and we highly recommend this being a key

part of your marketing plan.

7. State Associations. Every state in the union has a state process serving association. They operate just like NAPPS in terms of representing the interests of their members, some of them work hard to lobby their interests with the state legislature or the county governments, and also to educate members on how to serve process or to pass along important information about changes or events within the industry. And just like NAPPS can be a good way to network with other servers in other parts of your state so that if they have a court document that needs to be served in your city, they'll call you to do it for them rather than drive across the state to do it themselves.

8. Door-to-door. This is perhaps the most difficult, time-consuming, and disheartening approach. You could visit law firms for hours, days, months ... and you might get one client using this approach. It is not totally hopeless, but it takes a lot of time and you will get a lot of rejection. A past associate of mine did just that when he got started in the business. It took a lot of effort, but he did land a client whom he has had to this very day, so that one time it did pay off.

9. Social media networking. There are a number of these organisms in existence on the internet and they are all the buzz these days when it comes to marketing your services. Facebook, Merchantcircle, and Linked-In, are just three of scores of social media networking sites and communities where you can connect with potential clients, other process servers, and businesses that might be in need of a process server. If you are not involved in the social media storm, then put on your galoshes, grab your umbrella and get out there. Why? Because now you have the potential of presenting yourself and your services to virtually anyone on the planet -- not just in your city or town. And in most cases, you can do it for nothing except a little bit of your time. Again, it is a numbers game, but if you made social media connections with 500 other process serving companies in the United States, it is likely that at least one or more will contact you to help them out in your area.

10. Now I am going to talk about one of those target specific demographics for obtaining clients. The state and national associations are great for networking and they can provide you that business-to-business client (i.e., another process serving company). But ask yourself this question: With whom do you interact the most

when working on a process serving assignment? Is it another process server? Sometimes. Is it the attorney who requested the court documents be issued? Sometimes. But who is it that you will communicate and interact with the most on each and every assignment you receive? And who is it that you must keep happy, make them look good, and basically keep problems out of their hair?

If you really want to narrow your focus and maximize your advertising and marketing dollars, then your client demographic are legal assistants and paralegals. Whether they typically work for plaintiff's attorneys or defense, if you target these individuals to become your clients, you will get more bang for your buck with the least amount of effort. The legal assistants at the plaintiff firms will obviously give you more assignments in terms of volume, but don't entirely ignore the defense firms. They sometimes have subpoenas to serve, sometimes they file court documents that counter-sue or enjoin a third party into a lawsuit. And legal assistants that work on the defense side know legal assistants in plaintiff firms, too.

So, how do you reach this market? Well, some of those ways have already been mentioned above, but another excellent way to meet and build lasting client relationships and friendships with legal assistants and paralegals is to become involved with their local, state, and national associations. Become a vendor member of their associations, and go to their meetings. You will probably find, too, that you will be the only process server there, so now you have virtually no competitors and a captive audience to boot. We are corporate members with the local legal secretaries association, and we have several members of that association that are now clients, and there are no other process servers or private investigators in that association. And the other corporate members present tend to be court reporting firms and records retrieval firms, which, by the way, can be another potential client. Check in your local community, and you are certain to find these associations, especially in large markets.

Local and state bar associations are another avenue, but these could be expensive to join and/or some are exclusive to attorneys. I have found, however, that bar associations do have events that you might be able to sponsor or attend, and some have newsletters for the members where you could advertise. For example, every year our company participates in a 5k run event with the local bar association. And every year we run side-by-side with current clients while meeting new attorneys and their legal assistants who are also running in the 5k event. Also, we have advertised in their newsletter on many occasions and obtained some very long term clients that way.

Customer Service

Although you might not think so, customer service is a part of, or at least a close cousin to marketing. After all, the key purpose of a business is not just to make money, but to obtain and keep a client. So customer service is critical, even when you are having a bad day. Remember, you are there to help the client achieve success in their own endeavors. You are there to provide good service and keep them out of trouble. You are there to solve problems and provide solutions. You are not there to create more, so do an excellent job and do it as quick as possible.

Customer service starts with communication. You must have strong communication skills and abilities if you desire even modest success. Now that does not mean that you need to be eloquent (although that would help), or have a vast vocabulary. No, communication requires, first, the ability to truly listen to the client. Don't just hear what they are saying, but really listen. And that requires your undivided attention with both ears. I heard it once said that you have two ears and one mouth. So wouldn't it be smart to listen twice as hard to your client's needs? And then provide a succinct solution for them. Take the problems they may be having, and are the reasons they are contacting you, and resolve them. Do it correctly, do it efficiently, and do it cost-effectively. But remember the key point here is not that you spoke, but rather that you listened.

Also, smile when you dial. Literally, try it. When you pick up the phone, actually smile. It will come across the phone conversation in your tone of voice and the client will intuit this. The reverse is also true. If you are having a bad day, trust me, they will know it, and that isn't always best for the relationship. And when you communicate through correspondence or email, be succinct, be grammatically correct, be polite, and be certain that you choose words that sound friendly, warm, and most importantly, that you are receptive to whatever it is they require of you as if you were chatting with a good friend.

Which brings up another issue. In the beginning I used to treat my clients just like that – a client. I was all business and very much to the point. But over time I learned that the best approach was not to exist in a vendor-client status, but rather to build rapport with the client and thereby create a relationship. Take the time to find out what their personalities are like, and what hobbies they enjoy. Become familiar with aspects of their personal life if they are willing to share. And trust me, they will if you are open and friendly and share with them those things about you that make you unique. When the time permits take yourself out of the professional mode with the client (while still maintaining a professional demeanor) and establish something lasting as if you were developing a friendship. Because, in fact, that is exactly what you will be doing. I do not even refer to my clients as clients when I correspond with them. I call them my friends, and that is very much how I feel about them.

Introduce, Involve, Increase (Upgrade)

This is all about growing sideways through your client base. Once you do have a client, a good way to get more business is to, firstly, do a great job for them, and then, secondly, keep them in the loop and engaged in the process (no pun intended), including educating them a little on what you are doing for them, and then, thirdly, increase the amount of work you do for them by introducing them to new, additional services. Same client, just offer a different service. It's what McDonald's does everyday.

It works like this at McDonald's. You come in and ask for a hamburger. The attendant asks if you want cheese on it. You say, yes. Then the attendant asks if you want fries. You say, yes. Then the attendant asks if you want a large order of fries. You say, yes. Then the attendant asks if you want something to drink. And you say, yes. In fact, the whole process with them has become so routine, that most people now walk into their restaurants and before the attendant can even ask if you want a hamburger with cheese and a large order of fries with a drink, the customer already knows what they are going to be asked, and they just spew it all out at once.

You can do the same thing in process service. How do you do that when all you are doing is serving a paper. Here's an easy example. Your client contacts you to serve a subpoena. And you respond by telling them that you can do that, and then you ask, do you want us to place a rush on that. And they say, yes. Or, you ask them, do you want me to prepare the subpoena (which under certain circumstances you can legally do), and they say, yes.

Here's another example. You may already know how to serve court documents, but you also know how to locate people who need to be served. This is called skip tracing. This is an additional service you can provide. Or perhaps you can offer to do courier service for the client, or act as a notary public for sworn documents. If you are qualified and licensed, you can also offer the client to do private investigations. Plenty of attorneys have a need for investigative services. If you are already working on their process service, it is easier to give you the investigations, seeing as they already know you, than for them to locate an investigator, get quotes, vet them, retain them, etc.

So, in that way you introduce the client to a new service, you involve them in the new service by providing quality customer service and education into the process, and then you increase the level of services by introducing yet another new or additional service. It could become an endless cycle if you could find an endless number of services to provide. You could start serving court documents for one client, but before too long, you could be serving the court documents, running investigations, locating witnesses, notarizing documents, completing courier deliveries, retrieving court records, researching court files, preparing subpoenas, and on and on and on.

Holiday Baskets & Goodies

Whether you have existing clients or someone nibbling on the postcard hook or it's stone cold calling, take some donuts, or some candy, or a nice basket with cookies. I do this quite often with my existing clients. It does two things if they are an existing client: it builds customer loyalty, and lets anyone else in that law firm who isn't a client, but sees the goodies you brought, want to be your client so they can get goodies on an occasional basis. If they are not a client yet, but you had received a call from them based upon a postcard you sent to them or an ad of yours they saw, then follow up on the call by making a visit with a sweet offering.

Most of the people you are going to be dealing with on a day to day basis are legal secretaries. Paralegals and legal assistants are predominantly female. What wonderful lady doesn't like chocolate? Or scented candles? Or cookies? Bubble bath soap? If they weren't a client, yet, by the time you leave the law firm, they will be if not for the simple reason they might feel a little obligated to return the favor of receiving a nice gift. Focus on the holidays; Halloween or Christmas or even Valentine's Day (especially, Valentine's Day).

Here's a perfect example of how it can work. A particular legal assistant at a law firm where I did not have clients had contacted me about obtaining a copy of a court document, which she knew I had retrieved a copy of for someone who was a client of mine on the other side of the lawsuit her law firm was working on. She just wanted to get a copy of the document and knew I could provide it as I had a copy already. Her firm was going to (naturally) pay for the copy, but that didn't mean at this point she was going to start using me to obtain court documents or serve legal process or conduct investigations for her on a regular basis, though. But I took this one contact and used it to my advantage.

I provided what she needed and sent it to her along with the invoice for providing it. A month went by and the invoice came up in my accounting system as having not been paid. I wasn't worried that I wouldn't get paid. Someone else might have, but I was familiar with the type of law firm she worked at and had a good feeling that it was merely an oversight by accounting department folks (which it was). I contacted her, and gently reminded her that the invoice had come up past due. I also made some small-talk with her, and was generally friendly in tone, then hung up and went about my day. A week later the invoice was paid. But that isn't the end of the story.

Since I had had some interaction with this legal assistant, I put her on my list for a goody basket for Christmas. I went to the firm in person and delivered a basket filled with the candy and cookies. Instead of being confronted by the receptionist as just another solicitor (with a scowl), I was instead welcomed (with a glowing smile). I introduced myself, said I had a basket for the legal assistant, and asked if she could come and get it so I could meet her.

As it turned out, the legal assistant wasn't in that day, but that was fine. I left the basket for her with her name on it and my business cards in it. Then six weeks later, Valentine's Day came up. I did the same thing. I delivered a nicely boxed Valentine chocolate from a very high-end chocolatier. The legal assistant was out to lunch, so again I couldn't meet her (honestly, my timing was simply off with this one).

On St. Patrick's Day, I went with a bag of goodies to help

celebrate that holiday. This time, I figured, I haven't received any work from her, or a thank you, or a phone call, and had not been able to meet with her, so I just left the bag of goodies, and figured this would probably be the last shot at it.

A week went by and I received a handwritten from her on the law firm's stationery. She told me how sorry she was for not having written sooner, or called to say thank you, but she was so happy for the goodies she had received over the last few months. In fact, she was most appreciative of the Valentine's Day gift as she was single and had been feeling gloomy on Valentine's Day until my gift showed up. I still have the letter to this day even though it was written years ago.

Subsequently, she called me to serve a subpoena for her attorney. Then another assignment came in -- and then another and another. Then another legal assistant in her law firm contacted me. She said she had been referred by the first and needed a citation served, and then she called again a few weeks later, and then called again, and again, etc. This went on throughout that law firm, which was a sizable office with a couple dozen attorneys.

To this day, I still receive a substantial number of

assignments from various legal assistants and attorneys in that law firm, and some of them have become good friends beyond being merely just clients. From that one opportunity and a little persistence combined with sweet bribery of the chocolate type, I was able to obtain a repeat client and a large stream of continuous income. That first legal assistant eventually left that law firm and went to another. She recommended me around the office of her new law firm. Then she moved on to another law firm and did the same thing there. I didn't even need to sell to these other law firms. She did the selling for me and all because I made her day ... one day ...Valentine's Day.

But why do this for existing clients? You might ask. You already have their business, why spend the time and the money? Two reasons: loyalty, and because I personally enjoy giving.

Look, your clients will be and are the only reason you are in business. Without them, you have no business. You have no income. You have no house, car, computer, phone, vacation money, groceries, or electricity. Take care of each one of them as if their assignments were the only ones you have in your hand. If you show them a little love, a little friendship, along with a competent service, they will be a customer for life. What's more, you will have such a good feeling in your heart when you see the look in their eyes once they get a nice gift for the holidays. You're giving back, you're saying thank you for the business they have given you which has allowed you to feed your family or make your mortgage payment. Show a little love and be grateful.

I am so thankful for the opportunity my friends (clients) have provided me by being of service to them because if they hadn't let me serve their papers, or retrieve their court documents, or investigate the matters involved in their lawsuits, I would be homeless ... or worse yet, working in a dead-end job for somebody else. They've given me everything and I rejoice in that. So it is the very least I can do to bring them a little something, even it is just a basket of cookies. And you should do the same thing with your existing clients because it is not a waste of time, or money, or energy. It is the continuance of a relationship with your customer and an expression of gratitude.

EQUIPMENT/SUPPLIES NEEDED

There is very little you can do without the right equipment these days. Now, if you have all the modern "toys", such as smart phones or a laptop and a wireless printer, that would be the optimum way to go if you are starting on your own without an office, or any employees, as once you start getting a book of clients, you will most likely be on the road throughout most of the day, and the wireless technology that is top of the line is the best way to go.

I have even heard of some servers who operate using a motorcycle, a notebook computer, a wireless printer, and a cell phone. They are completely mobile, can go anywhere cheaply and don't have to stop anywhere to pick up their assignments in most instances. You could receive contact from a client who already has the court documents in their office, and you can tell them to scan and email the court documents to you. You print out the court documents, and then go right away to serve them.

Now, that doesn't mean that's all you need to have a fully functioning business as at some point you might have someone who still needs to fax something to you, or you may need to copy or scan some documents yourself. So, having this additional equipment may be necessary at some point. But still, as the technology advances -- and it is advancing at a rapid pace -- it is becoming increasingly easy to quickly and efficiently execute process throughout the country. So, always remember, if you can afford it, technology is our friend. Repeat this mantra, "technology is our friend."

Of course, it is not necessary to have everything up front when first starting out. Our company began with a single desktop computer, a printer, a fax machine, a cellular phone, a traditional phone, and a functioning automobile. That was it in the beginning. But some people think it is necessary to buy every new toy out there and to get the latest and greatest technology. And I agree, as I have learned that technology is our friend. There's nothing wrong with all the "bells and whistles" if you can afford it. In fact, the most up-to-date computer technology would be wise to invest in as given the rapid pace at which computers become obsolete (usually within three years or less), buying the newest thing is the best thing to do.

But, even though technology is our friend, if you are just starting out, have a limited amount of finances, or if you have bad credit (something I suggest you repair if you are going to operate a business), then just start with the bare minimum and take what you can get just to be able to function. Then later, when you begin to achieve a level of revenue from the company that allows you to upgrade, or you are required because of the volume of work being received, then that's when you should assess the need to acquire better systems (management software) and equipment to operate the business.

If you have no funds to start with, then work with what you have. And process serving is one of those professions where you could get along without all the "bells and whistles". Although it would be difficult, you could probably operate as a process server, without any equipment whatsoever, actually, with the exception of a functioning phone and a moving motor vehicle. Yes, if you cannot afford even a computer, you could operate a process serving business ... at least in the beginning. It would be difficult and you would not be very competitive, but you could get moving and start obtaining clients, start serving papers, and start making money. So, there are no excuses.

Now, provided you have some funds, **here is the suggested bare minimum equipment items you should have if you want to have a business in process serving that will bring in clients, look professional, operate competitively, and complete assignments efficiently:**

Any computer with internet access

A printer – preferably laser black and white

Fax machine

Cell phone

Desktop copier

A functioning, preferably fuel efficient, vehicle

Basic office supplies – paper, envelopes, staples/stapler, paperclips, pens

Here's the equipment you should have once you really get going and want to run with or ahead of the pack:

Wifi – to receive assignments or contact by email while on the road

Portable printers – to print assignments in your car as you go

Cell phone - iPhones/Blackberry/smart phone

Copier

A functioning, very fuel efficient, vehicle

Conventional phone line or even an internet phone

A seriously big desk space

Fax machine

Postage meter

Business Cards

Office supplies - paper, envelopes, paperclips, staples, staplers, toner, folders, pens, mailing labels, whiteout, adhesive tape, etc.

High speed scanner

Forms to use for various office tasks – faxing, correspondence, field sheets, maps

Field equipment – binoculars, flashlight, clipboard, pens, note pad, water bottle, contact cards, vehicle phone charger

There are many other articles and items of equipment and supplies that you might need at one time or another, and the above lists are certainly not all-inclusive, but this should be enough to get you up and running, keep you profitable and competitive, and start you on down the road to running a respectable process serving company.

DRESS AND APPEARANCE

Okay, this topic is sometimes debated amongst my peers – dress and appearance. Some dress up. Some look about as slovenly as possible. And most others are somewhere in between. I have done all three depending on the situation.

In the beginning days, I spent a great deal of time going from law firm to law firm in between serving papers, and so I wanted to present a nice professional appearance. This worked great for getting the clients. I looked like a business professional. But it was not so great for serving papers, depending on the type of person I needed to serve. If I was going to serve a paper at a business, then having a tie was suitable. But if I was going into a neighborhood, the tie needed to go. Over the years as I was able to gain a little bit of recognition with regular and prospective clients, I was able to dress a little more on the casual side. Perhaps a pair of nice jeans without holes in them, etc., and a polo shirt sufficed. At least that way I could pass for a neighbor when knocking on a stranger's front door. I have tried the "it's Sunday afternoon and I am about to kick back with a beer look" before. You know, the t-shirt with the shorts and tennis shoes. Some process servers go that route everyday, Monday through Friday. But depending on how casual you get and the type of person you are about to serve, that look may not be helpful. Why? Well, let's say you go into a more "upscale" neighborhood. If you look like a homeless person standing at the door, or a groupy from a Megadeth concert, the middle or upper class housewife inside the residence may not be so willing to open the door to find out what you want. Secondly, if you come to a gated community with a security guard, it is possible they may not let you in, or perhaps could give you some resistance even if you have some form of identification, simply based on your appearance. This also holds true for businesses and/or law firms that you might visit to serve court documents.

So, just keep in mind, casual is best. Try to fit in under the circumstances you know you will be entering. Be non-threatening and professional-looking and a lot of doors will open for you.

FINANCES AND TAXES

Although the subject of business taxes and financial considerations may seem complicated, it is an area that can, if understood, be made reasonably simple, and, in my opinion, is critical to the success of your business even in its early stages.

One of the first things to consider is obtaining a tax identification number for the business. This is a separate number used by the Internal Revenue Service that applies to business entities, and is oftentimes requested of from your clients in order for them issue payment to your company. I have seen some small companies and sole proprietors operate without a tax ID, but then that often requires them to provide their personal Social Security Number for purposes of payment from their clients. This is not exactly what I would consider presenting a professional image if your intention is to present yourself as a professional company. That and you run the risk of someone obtaining your SSN and using it for nefarious purposes. You can obtain a tax ID number by contacting the IRS and providing the proper forms to have it issued for your company.

Now, once you are up and running and begin generating revenue, this ultimately leads to taxation from the income derived from the business. As a company, you will have to pay quarterly income taxes to the IRS, and the amount paid will depend on how much income you are generating from the business and this could vary from one year to the next. You could pay annually (on April 15th), but you might want to consult a good accountant about that as there could be additional fees or penalties for doing this as opposed to paying quarterly.

Now, when it comes to calculating and paying income tax for the business or yourself, at first, it might be okay to do your own taxes. But as the company grows, the expenses, the allowable tax write offs, the tax laws, and regulations all become increasingly more complex and if not done properly can lead to trouble with the government. The key here is not to get in trouble because you do not understand the tax laws, or you become insolvent or unprofitable because you did not maximize the amount of allowable tax write offs. I cannot stress this enough. A certified public accountant, even in the beginning, would be the best thing you could do to keep yourself out of trouble and maximize your tax savings benefits.

Many people believe the tax code is written in such a way as to be a hindrance to a business owner, but the reality is that if you know and understand the current tax code, it is actually geared toward providing considerable benefits to businesses and investors in businesses. The tax codes can actually be your best friend if you know how to use it. And the operative words here are "if you know how". Most of us do not, including me, but my CPA knows. Although I have to pay for this service, it is a wise investment, and one, by the way, that is always an expense that can be written off as well.

Quickbooks for accounting is another product worth considering. In the beginning it might be okay to use a regular bank ledger to keep track of income and expenses, but Quickbooks software is an excellent way of keeping track of those things as well providing you with profit and loss statements (which are important when it comes to completing income tax returns for the business), calculating contract labor costs for Form 1099s (which you will have to complete if you hired another process server to handle assignments for you), and categorizing your various expenses which your accountant will need in order to properly complete your income tax returns at the end of the year. The expense for purchasing Quickbooks software is minimal, and the set up time is negligible, but the pay off in terms of time savings when it comes to the financial aspects of your business is golden.

The last thing to consider in terms of the financial aspects of running a process service company is insurance. Although it may not be required that you carry some form of liability insurance to serve court documents, it would not be a bad idea, either. Consider this: If you start out as a sole proprietor, basically what that means is that you have an assumed name, but the company is still you, really. Now what if something happened while in the performance of serving papers in which you accidently injured someone, or caused some sort of property damage, or in rare instances made an error or mistake in completing or filing a return of service? Who's liable for the damages? You are the company, so even if only your company is sued you are still personally exposed to the loss. Any assets you have could be rendered following a judgment on that lawsuit depending on the state you reside and how the laws apply. Even if you are not required by law to obtain some form of insurance to serve process, you should obtain a policy. Yes, it is another business expense, but again, it is a tax write off, and one that could keep you from losing everything.

KEEPING TRACK OF THINGS

Although there are many things in this book that are important and critical if you wish to reach success, this next topic is the key to everything.

Organization.

If you are organized and things are properly planned out ahead of time, even those unexpected events that come up almost daily in the process serving industry can be managed with ease. If you stay organized and have everything in its proper place at all times, you will find that you can run a process serving business all by yourself, keep things from spiraling out of control, and run things smoothly and efficiently.

What I am about to suggest to you in terms of how to do this is heavy on the need for keeping a competent filing system within the office. This system may not be the only way to get organized and stay organized, but I found that it worked for me, and once you understand it, then it just might work for you. If after looking at what I am suggesting here does not look like your "cup of tea", then at least consider the implications of what an organized filing system might do for you in terms of managing your business and then adopt your own system. I am merely showing you one of many ways you could streamline and manage things so that you can run the business and the business does not run you.

One of the most difficult things I found to do was to keep track of the status of pending assignments, especially those that I had sent out of town for service through another process server. I would be busy with the assignments I had visibly in front of me, and so as the saying goes, "out of sight, out of mind." Then one of my clients would call wanting to know the status of their assignment – you know, that one that I had sent to another server in California or Michigan. And I really did not like telling a client I did not know whether their paper was served or not, and the second thing I did not want to say was that I would have to check and call them back. Instead, I would prefer to tell them, I know the paper is not yet served and here are the reason(s) why, or, yes, that paper is served. So, I started using a follow up filing system. You can try this out for yourself and see if it works for you.

The key to this filing system is what has been termed a "tickler file". The tickler filing system is set up as follows, and can fit within a single drawer of any small filing cabinet, and it is arranged/constructed as a physical method by which to conduct updates, make status checks with the servers and with clients, and keep the flow of assignments moving without allowing any assignment or other matter to linger for a protracted period without being addressed or at least monitored. It is set up on a calendar cycle where you have 31 folders (one for each day of a typical month, and then an additional twelve folders (one for each month of the year). So, take 31 folders, label them one through thirty-one, and then take twelve more folders and label them each with the twelve months of the year – one folder for January, one for February, one for March, etc.

As assignments and other matters come into existence, physical document reminders will then be composed by you which you will place in these various folders, such as printing an extra copy of your individual assignment fieldsheets or you can use just a plain piece of paper and print the name of the defendant being served, and then place this physical document into one of the numbered file folders as deemed appropriate.

For example, if you receive a routine process serving assignment, then the extra copy of your assignment fieldsheet should be placed into the appropriate numbered folder three business days out from the date that assignment was received by you (or you could place it two days out or five days out, depending on how quickly you want to follow up on the assignment).

You may be scratching your head about this, so here is a more detailed example. If you received a court document for service that needed to be served in another city and you locate another server, and then send the assignment out to them, you may want to know three or four days later whether they received the court documents, and/or if they have attempted service yet. So, say you received the court document and sent it out on the 2nd day of March. Then take a piece of paper or an extra copy of your fieldsheet you sent with the court documents to the other server and place that in the number "5" folder (provided that the 5th of March is a business day). Now when it is the 5th of March, you open up the number "5" folder, pull out the piece of paper with whatever information you have on it regarding the assignment, and you now have a physical reminder to check on the assignment with that out-of-town server.

To take this a step further, let's say now that you begin to take on more and more assignments. As this occurs over a matter of days and weeks, you will place these physical paper reminders into the various numbered folders. And then, each day you will open up whatever numbered folder the day of the calendar it falls on and there is your physical reminder to check on the assignment. If today is the 11th of May, then open up the number 11 folder and pull out the paper(s) in there, and then make a phone call or send an email to find out what is going on with the service of your court documents by that out-of-town process server. It is as easy as that.

The same goes for the twelve monthly folders as well. Let's say you have an assignment or some other project that may need a little more time to work on before you are required to check on it. The monthly folders are there for that purpose.

Here's an example of how this would work. Let's say you have a court document that you started working on yourself, and then the client called you and asked that you stop attempting to serve the court document until further notice, and to just hold on to it. This does come up on occasion, and it is likely that you might eventually go back to attempting service on the court document, but for now the client wants you to hold on the service. This would be a perfect time to place the actual assignment in to a "holding folder" (we'll get to that in a moment), and then place a physical reminder such as an extra copy of your assignment field sheet in one of the monthly folders that is, for example, the following month.

In other words, let's say today is February 15th, and the client contacts you to hold the assignment. You just don't want that assignment to sit there for months without checking with the client at some point, but you also don't want to be calling them every week to find out whether to continue to hold or not, either. So, plan to follow up in thirty days by placing the extra fieldsheet in the March folder. At least that way, there is still that reminder available to you a month or so later. And trust me, it does happen that you are asked to hold on an assignment, and then if you do not follow up on it, a few months could go by before you realize this assignment has been sitting there. You then contact the client, and sure enough, the client tells you they completely forgot about it themselves, and the matter settled weeks ago, so you need to non-serve the court documents. Well, that meant you were sitting there with a court document that no longer needed to be served, and you have already worked on it, so you are entitled to invoice for the work, but you could have done that weeks or even months ago.

Now, you might ask, why do I use an actual physical filing system? Can't I just set up reminders on my smart phone or on my computer, etc.? The answer is, yes, you can do that. You can set this system up electronically if you so desire, but you might find that actually having a physical document in front of you each day may be much more desirable. There is something psychological about having a material, physical instrument in front of you that works far better as a reminder. Some people work well with electronic reminders or calendars, but what if you are the forgetful type or you drop out of the habit of looking at your calendar on your phone or computer? A few days slip by and then all of a sudden a client calls checking on status and you have completely forgotten about it. But if that physical folder is sitting right in front of you everyday, and you pull out a physical piece of paper everyday from one of those folders, you won't forget about what is staring you right in the face. Also, what happens if your electronic filing system crashes? For instance, you lose your smart phone or your computer breaks down. Well, there went your filing system, too, and all of the data reminders if you failed to make a back up of things. With a physical filing system, the only thing that can happen to it would be a result of your office being destroyed or otherwise damaged by fire, flood, tornado, hurricane or earthquake, and if that happened, you would probably be far more concerned about other things than with the status of pending assignments or projects.

Again, I am not proposing that this is the only way to keep organized and/or that it is all-inclusive. But it is a way to keep track of things, and I have used it myself for many years. There may be different ways to do it. There may be better ways to do it. But for those of you who have trouble with keeping things organized and do not have any idea how or where to get started, then this is just one suggestion that might work for you.

Another key part of this physical filing system that goes beyond keeping track of assignments is a set of specialized folders. Again, these physical folders are where you will put physical things into them so you can keep track of where they are at all times. I call them Daily Folders, and they help with managing various tasks that need to be done on a daily basis.

The first one is a Follow Up folder. Wait, I just set up thirty one folders for that, why do I need yet another one? This one folder is an offshoot of the tickler folders, and here is how it works. Let's say you pull out all the physical reminders from tickler folder number 23 (because today is the 23rd day of whatever month). There are several reminders (fieldsheets, etc.) in there, too. And then you also have some other reminder notes that have nothing to do with checking on the status of an assignment(s). For example, let's say you had missed a phone call the previous afternoon and you need to return it. Any missed phone calls, especially from a client, should be written down on a piece of paper and placed in this daily follow up folder. What if you received an email the previous day, but did not have time to respond to it then. Well, print out a copy of the email sent to you and place it in this folder, so that the following morning when you do have time to respond to it, you will have a physical reminder to do so. There may be other things you might want to follow up on, so put a physical note of it in this folder so it will remind you to follow up on it.

The next folder you might want to have is a skip trace folder. If you offer that sort of service in conjunction with serving process, then this would be a great place to put those assignments where you need to run a skip trace to find a more current address to serve the defendant. If you do not offer skip trace services to your clients or you do not know how to do this, the folder is still good to have as it sets those assignments apart from the others you are still actively working on. You can keep those assignments there, and then let your client know about the bad address so that they can run a skip trace themselves, and then you can resume serving the paper at the new address without wondering where you put the assignment.

The next folder I would suggest having is a Special Projects folder. This is one in which you put physical reminders on paper of certain projects that are typically long term or they can be projects that might not be process serving related, but are certainly items necessary to be completed for the proper operation or continued progression of the business. For example, you might put reminders in this folder about working on gathering together certain files that your accountant needs in order to complete the tax returns, or you might be working on developing a new type of service to offer your clients, and this would be a good place to keep reminders about the project(s) so that they stay in the forefront of things and not be neglected.

The last daily folder to have is one that will typically have only one document in it. This is called the Goals Folder. The Goals Folder will have one document in it that is a list of at least ten business and personal goals you have written down which you would like to complete during the course of the year. You draft this goals document at the beginning of the year, and then everyday, you open this Goals Folder, and read those goals to keep you focused on whatever your goals might be for the coming year. That may sound unnecessary, but if you are really want to succeed in business, or for that matter in life overall, written goals, both personal and professional, are paramount.

And remember, the key to these daily folders, is to open them up "daily" and look at the documents that are inside them. Failure to do so may mean follow ups might be forgotten, special projects do not get completed, skip traces are not performed, and goals are not met.

There will be other types of files and folders you might want to set up, but here are a couple of others we maintain in our filing system for organizational purposes, which have been helpful.

Substitute Service File: In the State of Texas, under our rules for method of service, we have the means by which to deliver court documents by substituted service. Most all states have this method of service, but the implementation of it varies from state to state. In Texas, if it is determined that we need to "subserve" the court documents, under the Texas Rules of Civil Procedure, a motion has to be filed by the attorney of record (your client), and then an order is subsequently issued by the court that allows you to complete the delivery of the court documents either by delivering them to another individual at the service address or by affixing the court documents to the front entrance of the residence or building located at the service address.

This is not typically a quick process, and may require a few days in which the assignment is held up pending issuance of the substitute service order from the court. While the assignment is being held, our office keeps a separate file drawer where we place those assignments in separate folders for each assignment in alphabetical order. This way the court documents can be readily accessed once the order has been signed, and we don't risk the possibility of the assignment becoming lost. Even if the assignment is sitting somewhere on your desk, if you can't find it, then it is lost. So, wouldn't it be better to know where it is all the time, every time, and thereby save you the time of searching through a pile of paperwork cluttered all over your desk (or worse, the front seat of your vehicle)? And by the way, you should have a document in your tickler filing system that reminds you to check at least monthly on these assignments that are pending substitute service orders, as sometimes it could take that long to get the order from the court.

Expense/receipt filing folders: This is set of folders where you place various receipts for purchases related to the business. You can categorize these as you desire, but basically the idea here is to be able to have, for example, a folder where you can place all of your fuel receipts, all of your equipment purchases/receipts, all the receipts for office supplies purchased, rent paid on office space (if you have an actual commercial office space), etc. It may not seem necessary, but if you need a particular receipt, wouldn't be quicker to search through one little folder specific to that sort of purchase for the business rather than searching through a stack of several hundred or even several thousand receipts?

Closed Assignments File: Once an assignment is completed, you may want to keep a copy of the executed return of service or other important documents related to the assignment just in case they are needed in the future. This occurs on occasion where you complete an assignment, and then the client contacts you six months later wanting a copy of the return of service and now you have a copy you can quickly give to them rather than having to go to the courthouse to obtain another copy. Worse yet, what if the court lost the return of service (I have seen it happen). If you had a copy of the return of service, then there is proof to some extent that the service was actually completed even though the court lost its copy. Also, whatever notes or other things that might have arisen during the course of serving a court document should be kept in this file as sometimes, many months later, you might have to explain with some detail what occurred during the service of any particular set of court documents, and it is much easier to refer to your stored notes, rather than your independent memory of events.

The last organizational tool I would suggest is to consider investing in specialized management software for process service. When you first get started in process serving you may be able to keep track of things on your own, and especially through the use of the tickler filing system as described above. But as your volume of work grows, so does the amount of paperwork you have to manage and the number of assignments as well. Being able to set up each service assignment quickly so that you can be able to have all the necessary particulars about the assignment, including who is the client, who is the defendant or witness, where is the paper to be served, the generation of affidavits and returns of service, field sheets, and invoices becomes far less complicated if you use one of the various process service management software tools available.

There are a number of them on the market, and they allow you to input the particulars of any assignment into the software, and then from there you can print out fieldsheets so that you can keep good notes on any particular assignment, they keep all the client contact information at your fingertips, generate affidavits that might be useful, and generate invoices once the assignment is complete. These software management tools can be a real time saver.

SETTING UP A DAILY ROUTINE

Starting out things might not be too hectic. Your main job once you have the business set up is to look for clients. One of the rules of business is that when you don't have a job, your job is to get a job. And so at first, all you might be doing is sending out postcards on a massive and rapid pace, networking in various associations, or setting up other forms of advertising and marketing. If you do not already have a client when you start the business then you have to begin marketing big time. As mentioned before, it's a numbers game as well as just being in the right place at the right time.

But once you start getting clients you will quickly find that the day can be anything but "routine", and after awhile you find yourself running out of hours in the day to get everything done. In fact, if you're not organized, process serving can become rather chaotic as it is not a business that lends itself easily to a structured day. There are rarely appointments set in this business as if you were running a massage therapy clinic, or selling life insurance, or even installing air conditioning units. Instead, the assignments come in, and sometimes they come in all at once, or at the least convenient moment, and then you have to scramble.

This was a major problem for me when our little business started bringing in a regular flow of process serving assignments. In fact, it got so out of hand that it was interfering with our investigations, our court document retrieval, and our "after-hours" family life, and vacations. When it starts interfering with family events and vacations, like so many small businesses encounter, it is very hard to remedy this. Process service does not generally operate on a "banker's hours" schedule. In fact, most of the assignments are executed after the banks are closed and most people are at home eating dinner or watching television.

Many start-up businesses outside of process service have to work long hours, but there are not many that operate on what I call a "fireman's standby" concept. You know, you are waiting for the next process serving assignment, and, in fact, you are actually eating lunch, right in the middle of taking the next bite out of your cheeseburger, when you get a call to drop everything, go pick up some court documents right this instant, and go deliver them to a defendant or a witness before the business day is over or else. Firemen live that sort of life. They're in the fire station, cooking spaghetti, playing ping-pong, and then there goes the alarm, and it's down the pole and off to the fire. And process serving can become like a constant battle to put out fires and there you are not quite organized to go from one fire to the other.

But it doesn't have to be that way. It took me some time, and some learning from others in my field, and also reading a lot of business organization books, and doing a lot of things, trial and error, until I figured out a way to satisfy most, if not all, of the numerous client demands that would come up in a single day, and still have my family time, my vacation time, and my sanity. It was not easy to do it, and in fact, if you are like most entrepreneurs, you will struggle with it psychologically. But in the end you will better for it, you're clients will be confident that you can get the job done, you will be more productive, make more money, have a better reputation, and get more referrals, too.

I spent several hours stretched out over many months developing a routine. I mean I actually sat down and analyzed everything I do on a daily basis, and thought of the best times to do these things, how to do them, how long it took to do them, and then blocked out chunks of time in order to do them. It works whether you are a "lone ranger" or if you have several process servers working for you.

To follow is the schedule I follow. It works for me, and it will probably work for you. If it doesn't, you can always modify it to suit your particular situation. But whatever you do, get organized and set up an actual schedule, even if it just generally sets up your day, it will give just the right amount of structure you might need. Tight time planning is critical for a successful business. The tighter your time planning is the better. If you can schedule things down even to the minute, then do so, as it will make things run so much better. If you don't, and then you have one too many clients running you from point A to point B, it won't be long before you run yourself into the ground.

Typical Daily Routine – 10 hour day for "full-timers" with a large book of clients

Serve assignments in the a.m.

Mail

Email

Logouts (closing out completed assignments)

Logins from the mail (setting up new assignments)

Serving POE assignments (serving at businesses and places of employment)

Going through the follow up folders/daily folders

Return phone calls

Do correspondence/affidavits/skips

Serve POE assignments

Daily court run (afternoon pick up of new assignments at the courthouse)

Log in courthouse pick ups

Log out completed assignments

Serve new assignments that have a residential service address

This is just an example of a typical routine schedule you can establish to make things run smooth for you. If you require a little structure in your workday, process service may not be the type of business for you if you fail to develop at least a generalized daily routine. You may not always be able to stick to the routine as process service often requires you to switch gears and go another direction based on the demands of the clients, but some structure is better than no structure at all, and you might even find that if you have a routine set up, and you stick to it, even when emergencies arise, you will be ready for them no matter where those emergencies might take you.

THAT'S A WRAP!

Hopefully, the things you've read about in this book will be of some help to you in starting your own process service business. The information is certainly not all inclusive but should give you enough guidance to help you obtain clients, achieve profitability, and keep you focused and organized. But don't stop here. Keep reading and keep learning from those around you, not just from other process servers, but from other business owners.

Had I known then (when I first started serving court documents years ago) what I know now it could have saved me considerable time and money, and it is my hope that the information imparted here will help you move forward quickly without having to spend years figuring it all out through trial and error (and error, and error).

There are tens of thousands of process servers throughout the United States and all over the planet. There are hundreds of thousands, if not millions, of court documents being served all at once on any given day. So the opportunity to make a very good income is there, especially if you do it smart, keep it organized, and never ever give up on your dreams.

Business Opportunities & Mentoring

We do offer through our company the opportunity to obtain a complete business system based upon the principals outlined in this book. For those interested we can provide you with a complete start-up kit to include databases, professional licensing, marketing materials, and on-line or personal mentoring. We also offer opportunities as field representatives for our company in certain geographic locations for those interested in a more flexible and affordable way to be a part of the process serving industry without the complications of running a full-time business. To inquire about these opportunities please contact us online at www.rtr-i.com or by telephone at 888-890-6762.

About the Author:

Bob Hill is a former special agent with the United States Air Force Office of Special Investigations, and is currently the owner of Record Time Retrieval & Investigations, LLC, which is a process serving and private investigative company located in San Antonio, Texas, with additional process serving locations in the Texas Hill Country region. Mr. Hill is also a licensed private investigator and certified private process server. He is a member of the National Association of Professional Process Servers, the Texas Process Servers Association, and the Texas Association of Licensed Investigators.

Made in the USA
Lexington, KY
05 October 2016